10 Guiding Principles of the Ethical Entrepreneur

How Mindset, Habits & Beliefs of the Business Professional Determine Long-Term Success

Co-Host of Bootstrap Businessmen

Kevin S Allen

Introduction

Guiding Principle 1: "Thou Shall Not Steal"

Guiding Principle 2: Respond Quickly Silence is Deadly

Guiding Principle 3: Be Tenacious

Guiding Principle 4: Serve Customers Over Profit

Guiding Principle 5: Under Promise and Over Deliver

Guiding Principle 6: Listen to Your Customers
   1. Individuals Have Needs
   2. What Do Customers Think of the Competition?
   3. Predict Future Customer Needs

Guiding Principle 7: Never Assume

Guiding Principle 8: Knowledge is Power

Guiding Principle 9: Have Integrity in Everything You Do

Guiding Principle 10: Put Loyalty to Work for You

Conclusion

Our Gratitude & Contact Info

Speeches & Workshops

About the Author

Introduction

With millions of entrepreneur books on the market, what makes *10 Guiding Principles of the Ethical Entrepreneur* any different? The majority of these books are filled with get-rich-quick, and make-money-fast schemes. However, this book doesn't embody either of those qualities. I'll teach you how to build and grow a business with honesty, integrity, and an unwavering focus on the client, not just the paycheck.

The best part of *10 Guiding Principles of the Ethical Entrepreneur* is that anyone can implement these core values into any business and personal relationship without any specialized training.

Becoming an entrepreneur can be challenging yet very rewarding. Being an entrepreneur requires hard work, dedication, and sacrifice. When you get caught up in chasing the money, we forget about the reason why we wanted to be an entrepreneur in the first place—to serve others or to make a difference. While the following principles will not guarantee monetary success, they will help you develop an honest business.

Guiding Principle 1: "Thou Shall Not Steal"

Though the phrase "Thou shall not steal" sounds a bit religious because it is one of the Ten Commandments, it is just plain and simple truth, regardless of your spiritual or religious beliefs.

When starting out as an entrepreneur, this one belief and mindset should be at the top of the list for you. Trust is difficult to earn, and it can be ten times harder to earn back once broken. When your customers trust you, they do it with their attention, money, and overall belief in YOU!

Have you ever seen an email stating a product will make you money overnight? Then, when you purchase the product you're left with no idea how to use it or never even receive it. These offers are everywhere on the internet and fill thousands of email accounts daily. There is a good reason why trust is hard to gain. People get bombarded with emails and phone calls presenting one thing but actually receiving another.

So, what is the cure? Provide upfront value and don't wait till someone gives you their hard-earned money. Do this first and you will start to build trust. First and foremost, you have to provide value so consumers know why they should invest in you. Remember, people work hard to make a living. When they spend their money, they are hoping for value and a product or service that will benefit them.

Be the one who delivers the value upfront and instills confidence in your client, so they know they aren't alone.

There are many ways your clients trust you with their credit card information, checks and so on. When a client buys from you, they are being vulnerable. Do not take this information and abuse it. Don't steal time, money, attention away from your clients. You want to create a lasting business relationship with raving fans.

As you write out your business goals, please put this at the top of your list. Hold yourself accountable to this moral and number one business principle. Do not steal from your clients and, trust me, they will reward you tenfold with their loyalty and referrals.

My first and primary business is in the credit card processing industry—talk about clients being vulnerable. I have access to their business checking accounts, social security numbers, home address, and birth dates. So, I have to develop a high level of trust when gaining their business. Believe me, they watch for any discrepancies in their account for the first few months. With this level of inside knowledge on many people, I know what I am saying with being honest and not stealing.

Guiding Principle 2: Respond Quickly Silence is Deadly

I just can't state it any better—respond quickly because silence is deadly. These words ring loud and true within the entrepreneur world. Customers don't just want to be heard, they want to know they're being heard.

Getting honest feedback is essential to businesses looking to improve their customer's experience. However, capturing the customers' feelings isn't always easy when you consider a vast majority of customers don't complain when they're unhappy. They believe it's a waste of time to provide feedback because the business simply doesn't care.

Here are a few ways to create dialogue and encourage open feedback:

1. Make sure you are available by phone and email.
2. Be quick to respond to customer issues.
3. Listen to what customers are saying, don't be clueless.
4. Make the effort to be friendly.
5. Get to know your customers and their history.

Allow the client to know and feel there is an open door for communication. When you foster candid communication, they will feel comfortable asking even the smallest questions. And, this type of feedback means you have gained their trust.

Guiding Principle 3: Be Tenacious

I have worked with many successful people who have attained the kinds of lives they had only dreamed about. Conversely, I have also worked with many people who are not anywhere near where they want to be in life. Many times those who are unsuccessful resent those who are successful. These jaded individuals believe that somehow success was handed to those who have achieved much.

Yes, they are successful. However, success wasn't handed to them! Most unsuccessful people don't embody the same tenacity as their counterparts. Many people who complain about their lack of success simply haven't persevered and been tenacious enough. When asked why they lack results, an excuse is soon to follow. Yes, there are exceptions on both sides, but I find this to be almost universally true.

If you are one who finds yourself dreaming of a better life, or looking at someone who has it made, I would ask you take a long, deep look inward and at your life. Figure out whether or not you have actually been tenacious in the pursuit of your dreams.

How long have you gone for it? Many people who achieve a lot, go for years before they attain what their hearts long for? So, how hard have you gone for it? Most people who get much have given up much, sacrificed much, and strive valiantly for what resides deep in their dreams. They just plain work hard!

Guiding Principle 4: Serve Customers Over Profit

Always serve your customers first over the profit. You create loyalty through this action alone. The need to constantly find new customers becomes less of a demand on your expenses, too. In fact, when you honor this principle, you manifest the 80/20 rule. I believe you will gain 80% of your profit from 20% percent of your current customer base. This goes to show you the importance of customer retention.

A study performed by the Harvard Business School came up with this conclusion:

> *"We showed that in industry after industry, the high cost of acquiring customers renders many customer relationships unprofitable during their early years. Only in later years, when the cost of serving loyal customers falls and the volume of their purchases rises, do relationships generate big returns. The bottom line: Increasing customer retention rates by 5% increases profits by 25%."*[i]

This is likely one of the reasons why unsuccessful entrepreneurs don't always have customer retention at the top of their mind. Unlike lead generation or customer acquisition, retention campaigns take relatively longer before producing results. When you publish a lead form or launch an ad campaign, you can easily see and measure the results. This isn't always the case in customer retention because it deals more with loyalty, relationships, and engagement, which yield results that are not immediately seen and are trickier to measure.

In business and sales, the thrill of catching that next big fish seems more exciting than working with current customers. The new guy is a fresh stream of income. But, don't get lost in chasing the dollar and forget your current customers.

If you start engaging and serving your customer's needs, then you will see your profits or money start to grow. When you treat people like they matter, especially in the times we live in where there are so many that treat people like a dollar sign, you will stand out. And, you will begin to create a loyal and profitable customer base. When you add value to your product or service and take care of the client, they are more likely to invest more in you and refer other people to you.

In short, if you provide value, and serve the needs of your customer, then the profit will come. If you chase the dollar and forget the needs of your customers, then you will always be chasing the dollar, like a dog chasing its own tail.

Guiding Principle 5: Under-Promise and Over-Deliver

We are all guilty of this at one point or another—over-promising and under-delivering. You just have to learn it's better to under-promise and over-deliver. We get into the mode of promising the world just to get the sale or new client. Over-promising will come back to bite you at some point as business starts to develop between you and your customer. Sometimes, we over-promise in such a vague way like, "Oh, by next week," just to smooth things over with the client. In reality, they may have been expecting and accepted a longer time.

For example, I experienced the same issue at a hotel and a service station recently. Although the hotel's menu promised room service would start at 6:15 a.m., when I called at 6:20 a.m., I was subjected to a tinny, tape-recorded message saying.

"Room service will be open at 6:30."

I'm a morning coffee drinker, the 15 minutes is no big deal, in absolute terms. But, the delay was bothersome in light of the promise. I *perceived* I was getting rotten service, and the frustration was further compounded by the hotel's high price tag.

Another experience I had was when I ordered an unusual-sized tire from a local service station. I was surprised and delighted to be twice-assured I could pick it up just four hours later. I was busy then, so I said I'd return the next morning and left the service station feeling much better about its unusually high gas prices, which appeared to be offset by its service responsiveness.

I rearranged the next morning's schedule, and popped in at 9:00 a.m. To my dismay, the tire hadn't even been ordered and my morning was officially shot. This story is one more example of a shattered expectation. And once again, the issue was the perception, not the absolute. I originally expected to get the tire service to take at least a couple days and was more than willing to wait.

In conclusion, set the expectations according to the client's needs and wants and then deliver above. Some say that this sets the bar low, and I disagree since you are setting the bar where it should be—according to the customer's needs. Establish honest expectations and then do your best to beat the deadline or deliver above the customer's expectations. Take your time with the details and place the expectations at the client level. Then, blow them away by overshooting the originally promised outcome.

Guiding Principle 6: Listen to Your Customers

In all my years of being an entrepreneur and hanging around entrepreneurs, I have seen some incredible success stories and tremendous failures. Both have a degree of commonality—they both set out to have a great business selling products or helping consumers. The one degree of difference was one listened to their clients' needs the other served their own needs.

The goal of any business is to make money, and that objective is easier to reach when we listen to our customers and understand what they want. The best way to serve our customers is by listening to what they tell us. Actively seek their point of view. Ask questions, conduct surveys, and get specific. More often than not, in the course of a conversation, a customer will divulge information that is vital to your overall success. Consider three areas related to customers:

1. Individuals Have Needs

People are looking to fulfill basic human needs with products and services that will improve their lives. Smart business executives listen to their customers. Executives understand exactly what people want, when they want it and what they will pay for it. They spend a significant part of the week visiting with customers so they can respond with superior solutions.

Business owners should invite all employees to regularly visit with customers, regardless of their assignments. With this collective knowledge, the entire company will be informed and united in what it takes to attract, engage, and retain loyal customers.

2. What Do Customers Think of the Competition?

Customers have a variety of choices when buying their products. They seek options from trusted friends and family. Experienced shoppers explore what others are saying on social media and online customer reviews. Your company's product may be just one of many choices. We benefit from listening to our customers' opinions about their level of satisfaction with competing products. Take the time to thoroughly explore what others are saying about your competition. What we hear might provide us with information critical to helping us deliver the best solutions.

3. Predict Future Customer Needs

An ability to know or predict what the customer will need is critical. The late Steve Jobs was not only incredibly effective at understanding what people want, but also at innovating and providing a product to meet the needs customers didn't even know they had. This unique ability was a huge contributing factor to his incredible success. Jobs not only knew the current needs and wants of people, but he also possessed the uncanny ability to foresee future wishes. What can we learn from Jobs? We should not be comfortable with current solutions. We should look to the future and do our best to anticipate where we might take our customers with innovative solutions.

Guiding Principle 7: Never Assume

In business as in life, we should never assume anything. If you do not know something or maybe the situation appears unusual, ask questions for a better understanding. This would be the same process when working with customers. Never assume they know about the product you are selling. Ask twice, so you and your customer have a clear understanding of how things work, when will they be billed, and other options for services. If customers know everything about you, you are giving them more reasons to buy and to keep coming back to you. Purchasing everything needed in one place saves the customer time, hassle, and money—three magic words to the everyday busy and cash-strapped customer.

You can't assume customers will always be there. Customers may come to you for years, but if you haven't paid attention to them and have taken their business for granted, they may go elsewhere for better service.

Also, don't assume your sales force is doing their job. Get frequent sales reports from your team to see if they are calling on current customers and making the necessary prospecting calls.

Don't assume you've got it right. Look at every aspect of your business from an objective point-of-view and fix what needs to be changed.

Don't assume things will remain status quo. The world is changing and you need to evolve with it. Look around at your business and take nothing for granted. View your business with fresh eyes and a new perspective.

Don't assume anything and know that nothing will remain the same. Always keep your customers front and center with your business. Appreciate them and in turn, they will continue to be loyal.

In summary, never assume your customer knows everything you offer or provide. And, never take clients for granted. It's easier to keep your current customers and even expand their spending with you if you cherish them and their business. Never assume your business will remain the same. Always be willing to learn, grow, and modify your approach in how you handle your customers.

Guiding Principle 8: Knowledge is Power

Knowledge is power. Information is liberating. Education is the premise of progress, in every society, in every family.
- Kofi Annan

Highly successful entrepreneurs are obsessed with their business. They have a strong desire to acquire in-depth knowledge about all aspects. If you are a knowledge-seeker, then you constantly search for new information and experiences to navigate your company in a highly complex business environment.

Starting and growing a business is a formidable task. The demands on the entrepreneur are many:

- Mapping the industry landscape
- Understanding what products and services to offer
- Raising capital
- Managing employees and customers
- Competing in a global economy
- Understanding that knowledge is a valuable asset
- Analyzing complex business environments
- Solving problems
- Selecting the best course of action
- And, staying ahead of the competition

Knowledge-seeking entrepreneurs assess and manage effectively. They have to make decisions in highly complex environments with incomplete information, which includes a lot of risks. Your ability to collect and process a lot of information gives you a better understanding of your environment. Whether you have to make a decision about releasing a new product or service, rolling out a new marketing strategy, or introducing a new production process. Try to understand the implications of the choices you face, calculate the inherent risk in each, and select the best course of action.

You have a superior insight into your customers' needs. Constantly driven to gather knowledge about the business environment, you should quickly recognize trends in consumer behavior and effectively reallocate organizational resources to address the changing customer expectations. This business practice turns your customers into advocates and generates higher revenue for your company.

In short, if you are a true knowledge-seeker, then you should never stop learning. Your ability to absorb knowledge and information gives your company a much higher chance of survival and growth.

However, I have some words of caution. As a knowledge-seeker, your intellectual curiosity may generate too many new ideas and insights. You might pivot from one idea to the next—sometimes too quickly—confusing your employees and customers. This can hamper day-to-day decision-making as teams grapple with repeated changes in direction and incoherent strategies.

Knowing how to differentiate between ideas that truly improve your business from those that do not is the key.

Select ideas that streamline and add value to your business. Avoid the lure of implementing every idea and insight without measured reflection.

Guiding Principle 9: Have Integrity in Everything You Do

Having integrity in everything you do is not merely a guiding principle in business, but also a solid guiding principle in life. If I could teach only one value to live by, it would be this:

Success will come and go, but integrity is forever.

Integrity means doing the right thing at all times and in all circumstances, whether or not anyone is watching. It takes courage to do the right thing, no matter what the consequences will be. Building a reputation of integrity takes years, but it takes only a second to ruin it. So, don't do anything that could damage your integrity.

It may seem like people can gain power quickly and easily if they are willing to cut corners and act without the constraints of morality. Dishonesty may provide instant gratification, but it will never last. I can think of several examples of people without integrity who are successful and who win without ever getting caught, which creates a false perception of the path to success that you should follow. After all, people could get results they want in the moment without integrity. Unfortunately, the dishonest by-product comes at a steep price with far reaching consequences. That person has lost their ability to be trusted as a person of integrity, which is one of the most valuable qualities anyone can have in life. Profit and power are temporary. However, profit in a network of people who trust you as a person of integrity is forever.

The value of trust people have in you is immeasurable. Everyone who trusts you will spread the word to at least a few associates and word of your character will spread like wildfire. Consistently building trust leads to growing an army of people willing to go the extra mile to help you. They simply know that recommending you will never bring damage to their own reputation. Yes, the value of the trust others have in you brings limitless opportunities and endless possibilities.

A word of advice to those who are striving for a reputation of integrity:

Avoid those who are not trustworthy.

1. Do not do business with them.
2. Do not associate with them.
3. Do not make excuses for them.
4. Do not allow them to entice you into believing that while they may be dishonest with others, they would never be dishonest with me.

If someone is dishonest in any aspect of life, then it's guaranteed he will be dishonest in most everything in life. You cannot dismiss even those little acts of dishonesty, such as the person who takes two newspapers from the stand when they paid for only one.

Others pay attention to those you associate with, and will judge you based on the character of your associates. Why is that? It is best explained by a quote my father often says when he is reminding me to be careful of the company I am keeping:

When you lie down with dogs, you get fleas.

Inevitably, we become more like the people we surround ourselves with day-to-day. If we surround ourselves with people who are dishonest and willing to cut corners to get ahead, then we'll surely find ourselves following a pattern of first enduring their behavior, then accepting their behavior, and finally adopting their behavior. If you want to build a reputation as a person of integrity, then surround yourself with people of good character and unbending integrity.

In summary, keep the company you want to reflect and project. Remember, building a reputation takes years, but only one act of dishonesty can destroy it. Dishonesty will eventually catch up to you. It may not be today, and it may not be for many years. Rest assured, though, at some point, there will be a reckoning.

Guiding Principle 10: Put Loyalty to Work for You

Success is the result of perfection, hard work, learning from failure, loyalty, and persistence.

Putting loyalty to work for you is the way you truly have long-term sustainable growth in your business. Some steps to building loyal customers who become raving fans include:

- Answer or return calls promptly - never put this off
- Hit home runs with your clients - some ways to do this are following up with them once in a while, send a card for holidays, birthdays, and make basic human connections with your clients
- Relationships are fundamentally paramount – contact a client that has nothing to do with selling them anything but more to just check in (maybe some fun emails like an event in their area, birthday wish or a virtual high-five)

Following the other 9 principles in this book leads us here—if you have built relationships, been honest, and delivered on your promises, then your clients are not only loyal but raving fans of you. This also helps create a long-term customer relationship that you and your client can count on.

When you have met the needs of your customers, then you can ask for referrals. If you follow these guiding principles, your loyal customers will have no issue with spreading the word and sharing your exemplary services.

Conclusion

Though the *10 Guiding Principles of the Ethical Entrepreneur* are common sense, practical concepts, this saying best serves why I wrote this book:

Common sense isn't always common practice.

I spent quite a few years working for a large corporation at a regional level and trained some of the most brilliant minds in the industry. And, every person I came in contact with were truly special and shared a great heart for their business and everyday practices. Every now and then, temptation would rear its ugly head, and they were faced with one path or the other. Do you take the path of least resistance for a quick payoff and disingenuous business practices? Or, should you go down the path of hard work, perseverance, and integrity?

Much like life, business isn't always easy and really shouldn't be. After all, if it were easy, then wouldn't everyone be doing it? And, wouldn't everyone be super successful billionaires? In reality, that is not what business or life is like. If you want to be successful in all realms of life, business included, then you should use the 10 Guiding Principles to direct you down the proper path. And, when you follow these simple guidelines, you most assuredly guarantee a business of lifelong prosperity, truth, and fulfillment.

Now, get out there and become the business professional you were born to be!

-Kevin S. Allen

Our Gratitude & Contact Info

Thank you for downloading our book. We hope you enjoyed it and found it insightful. If it wouldn't be a bother, could you post an honest review of this book . We read all of our reviews and appreciate the open feedback so we continue to provide better books for you.

We're not all about selling you books—we do want to see you use what you've learned to build a greater life. As you work toward your goals, you may have questions or run into some issues. We'd like to help you, so let's connect. We don't charge for the assistance, so feel free to connect through any of the facets below:

On the web:

BootstrapBusinessmen.com

Like us on Facebook:

http://www.facebook.com/bootstrapbusinessmen

Follow us on Twitter:

http://www.twitter.com/bootstrapbiz

Follow us on Instagram:

http://www.instagram.com/bootstrapbusinessmen

Thank you, again! We hope to hear from you and wish you the best.

-Bootstrap Businessmen

Kevin S. Allen

Speeches & Workshops

The 10 Guiding Principles for the Ethical Entrepreneur
Workshop or Keynote

What if you could dramatically improve your success rates at work through simple cues and mindset shifts? And, wouldn't it be nice to learn from the best, most successful small business owners in the world?

The 10 Guiding Principles for the Ethical Entrepreneur with the Bootstrap Businessmen

Bootstrap Businessmen speak around the world at leadership meetings, business conferences, and executive retreats. Based on their book, *10 Guiding Principles for the Ethical Entrepreneur*, and on their professional experiences, Dale L. Roberts and Kevin S. Allen share the incredible ways anyone can achieve their greatest breakthroughs and triumphant successes.

To invite Bootstrap Businessmen for speaking at your next event,

email bootstrapbusinessmen@gmail.com

Or call 614-568-3658

About the Author

Bootstrap Businessmen is a bi-weekly show on developing the entrepreneur within. Go to Bootstrap Businessmen website for live and on-demand episodes with hosts Dale L. Roberts and Kevin S. Allen.

My name is Kevin S. Allen, and I have been an entrepreneur for the last 10 years of my life. I believe if you want more out of life, then you have to work for it and get it yourself. I'm a professionally trained Sales and Coaching leader who enjoys spending time with my wife and daughter, traveling, golf and being able to help others find their true path in life.

GET YOUR FREE GIFT

You've read the book *Fail to Succeed: 5 Mindset Principles to Personal Growth* yet do you crave more information? What if we told you the mistakes you make affect your long-term success? And, wouldn't it be terrible if you failed the wrong way in your journey to victory?

Then, *The Terrible Ten: 10 Habits Destroying Your Success* has your answers!

Bootstrap Businessmen hosts Dale L. Roberts and Kevin S. Allen provide this short report that doubles as a checklist of what NOT to do when you're trying to capitalize on your failures. This eBook is completely free for new subscribers to the Bootstrap Businessmen newsletter.

Go to Fail.BootstrapBusinessmen.com

for your free report TODAY!

CLICK_HERE_TO_GET_YOUR_COPY

to 95 1 Amanda Stillwagon Smallbiz Trends Sept 11 2014 in Sales

www.ingramcontent.com/pod-product-compliance
Lightning Source LLC
Chambersburg PA
CBHW061235180526
45170CB00003B/1311